N. C. Denson

The Life and Times of
Reverend N. C. Denson

Reminiscences of a Confederate soldier,
dedicated minister, and Arkansas leader

Compiled and edited by
Dillard Denson, M.D.

Dillard Denson, M.D.
8 Rebanar Lane
Hot Springs Village, AR 71909
dillarddenson@aol.com

ISBN 978-0-9838992-4-2

Cover photograph: Reverend Nicholas Council Denson
    holding the cane he was given by the Arkansas State
    Senate in 1905

Book and cover design: H. K. Stewart

Printed in the United States of America

This book is printed on archival-quality paper that meets requirements of the American National Standard for Information Sciences, Permanence of Paper, Printed Library Materials, ANSI Z39.48-1984.

To Larry Dennis Curbow

*His encouragement, support, and enthusiasm
have made this book possible.*

Introduction

$\mathcal{T}$he first Denson who came to America was William Denson, who came from Bristol, England, in 1637 and worked as an indentured servant of Robert Pitt, Isle of Wight County, Virginia, for seven years. For the next two generations, the Densons lived on the Nansemond River in Virginia. For the next several generations, the Densons lived along the Pee Dee River, Anson County, North Carolina.

Nathaniel Denson, Sr., who went on to become a Baptist minister, was born around 1770 in Anson County, North Carolina. He married Charity Colson around 1784, and they had eleven children: James (1791-1839), Isaac (b. 1793), Joseph (b. 1795), Jesse (b. 1797), William J. (b. 1800), Thomas C. (b. 1802), Mary (b. 1804), Katharine (1807-1878), Shadrach (b. 1809), Nathaniel, Jr. (b. 1811), and Madison (b. 1815). The Densons settled in Alabama in the early 1800s and then moved near Sand Hill in Rankin County, Mississippi, in 1827, founding Denson Town, which later became known as Denson's Landing.

Nathaniel, Sr.'s, son William J. followed in his footsteps and also became a Baptist minister. Known informally as

"Parson Bill," William married Mary Jane Williams in 1826. After moving to Mississippi, the Densons had two children, Mary Jane (b. 1830) and David W. (b. 1832). Around this time in 1831, Mt. Pisgah Baptist Church was founded near Sand Hill, making it one of the oldest Baptist churches in the Mississippi area, and Parson Bill became its first pastor. His brother Jesse Denson was a deacon and church treasurer for a number of years. The church first met in the home of another brother, Nathaniel Denson, Jr. A few years later, William Denson donated six acres of land near Sand Hill and helped build the first church on the site in 1836, which became known as "Old Pisgah." It was the second Baptist congregation to be formed in the county. The original church was built of bricks made by yet another brother, Joseph Denson. It was a one-story building with a balcony for slaves. The Mt. Pisgah Baptist Church building was moved four miles south to its present site in 1857.

Another of Reverend Nathaniel's sons, Isaac, left Denson Town in the mid-1840s and moved his family to Arkansas to land he had been given for serving in the War of 1812. Taking both his son Albert and grandson Nicholas C. Denson, Isaac made the long trip westward across the Pearl River and then across the Mississippi River around St. Charles, Louisiana, then north to Fountain Hill in Ashley County, Arkansas, where they finally settled. Several of his brothers stayed behind in Rankin County, including Parson Bill, Joseph the Giant, and Jesse the Scribe, all of whom are buried in the Old Pisgah Cemetery near Sand Hill along with their father, Nathaniel, Sr. Joseph the Giant (1795-1844), who also fought in the War of 1812, was 6'8". On his return to Denson Town, he helped his neighbors herd their cattle by lifting a fully grown cow over a fence to change pastures. And Jesse the Scribe was the personal secretary of General Andrew Jackson in the War of 1812 in the Battle of New Orleans.

Isaac's grandson Nicholas C. went on to serve his own stint in a much larger war and then returned to become a Baptist minister in south Arkansas where he grew up. Here in his own words are the life and times of Reverend Nicholas C. Denson, which he dictated to his daughter Lucy Denson Daniel, regarding his life growing up in Fountain Hill, Arkansas. It tells of his military service in the Civil War and his dedication to 50 years in the ministry.

Reminiscences of the Reverend N. C. Denson

Written by Request of Loved Ones and Dedicated to My Youngest Daughter, Lucy Denson Daniel

I was born May 13, 1841, in Rankin County, Mississippi. My father was Albert C. Denson, and my mother was Emily Eley Denson. In the winter of 1844 and 1845, I moved with Father, Mother, Brother, and two sisters, Cassandrie and Emily Denson, to Arkansas and settled in what is now Fountain Hill, Ashley County, Arkansas. Another brother, R. L. Denson was born in August 1846. Father died February 25, 1847. Mother married again in 1851 to P. H. Baldy. From this union three children were born: Edward B., Betty, and Joseph Baldy. Mr. Baldy had children at the time of their marriage: Rebecca, Thomas, William, Samuel, Mary, James, and Rachael. At this writing, March 23, 1916, all have passed to the other shore except brother R. L. Denson of Fountain Hill, Arkansas, Betty Baldy Nix Barzona, and T. H. Baldy of Gatesville, Texas.

I was reared on a farm near Fountain Hill, Arkansas. What school advantages I had were at Fountain Hill Academy. Professed religion August 13, 1856, and was baptized August 17, 1856, into the Fellowship of Flat Creek Baptist Church by Bernafe Carroll. In the early part of January 1858, left home to battle and grapple with the problems of life. Lived first with Uncle Montgomery Denson. Made a crop and worked for a part of the crop. In August sold my part of the crop to Grandfather Denson and hired to Uncle Madison J. Denson for $12.50 per month. But in November at the earnest solicitation of Grandfather Isaac N. Denson, I went with him to Columbia County, Arkansas, where I worked on his farm until May 1859. I entered school with B. W. Bourland as teacher.

In December I returned to Ashley County where I entered into co-partnership with brother N. E. Denson to farm, our stepfather, P. H. Baldy, having agreed to turn over a few Negroes, one man, three women, and three boys. We build a few cabins on a tract of land belonging to cousin Madison Denson. Bought two horses, one for $125.00 and the other for $120.00 on credit. We rented land up and down Flat Creek for two or three miles adjacent to the northeast corner of Fountain Prairie where we worked days and parts of nights. Made a good crop of cotton and corn. Sold for good price and paid debts.

Entered 160 acres of land one mile west of Fountain Prairie, built a boxed house with two rooms and porch, two Negro cabins, pole crib, and stable. Cleared about 40 or 60 acres of land the first winter, '60 and '61. Set up housekeeping with two brothers, two sisters, and a few Negroes. As I was physically stronger than my older brother and my younger being young, the old Negro man being old, and the Negro boys young, I took the load in splitting rails to fence the ground and deadening timber, cutting the oaks through the sap.

Having a great desire for an education, I agreed with my older brother that one of us would work on the farm and the other go to school. So in April '61 I started to school at Fountain Hill Academy. W. F. Mack was the teacher. But after six weeks of school, the war between the States came on.

Believing it a duty to home and loved ones, I agreed to go with the first company that left Hamburg, June 1, 1861, on foot for Virginia. We had about 100 mostly young men and boys. Our officers: Captain, Van H. Manning; First Lieut, W. J. Wilkins; Second Lieut, J. W. Morris; Third Lieut, B. F. Lowe. None of my officers ever resigned. First Sergt, J. W. Manning, brother to the Captain. After three days' marching with a ride of seven miles on a railroad, we reached Guice, on the Mississippi River. After a few hours' wait, we got transportation on a steamboat to Memphis, where we went by railroad to Lynchburg, Virginia. Arriving at Lynchburg June 12. About the first of July we were organized into a regiment known as the Third Arkansas Infantry.

Albert Rust, Col.; Lieut Col. Barton. Capt. Manning was promoted to Major and J. W. Wilkins to Captain. J. W.

Morris, First Lieut.; B. F. Lowe, Second Lieut.; and W. W. Cochran elected as Third Lieut. We left Lynchburg July 17, by way of Stanton, for West Virginia. We were close enough on the 21st to hear the cannon at the First Battle of Manassas, or Bull Run. At Stanton my stepbrother Sam Baldy, a member of Company C, lost his footing, fell, and was killed by the car wheels.

❧

Civil War Casualty

N. C. Denson wrote the following letter only one month and 18 days after leaving Hamburg, Arkansas, on June 1, 1861, to fight in the Civil War. It reports what was probably the first war casualty from the first contingent of soldiers from Hamburg, the death of his stepbrother Sam.

He wrote the letter to his stepfather to inform him of Sam's death, but it is obvious that he meant for the letter to be shared with his mother, siblings, and his friends. Isac (Isaac), who was mentioned in the letter, was N. C.'s first cousin and was later killed in combat.

The Letter

Stanton Va. July 18, 1861
Mr. P. H. Baldy

Deare Sir, It affords me the greatest of pleasure to write you a few lines but Deare Father while it affords me the greatest of pleasure to write you a few lines it is with reluctance and sadness that I pen you the following lines. Friends read these few lines with prayerful hearts and with firmness. On the evening of the 17th about seven o'clock S. S. Baldy departed this life, but Deare Father while it grieves my heart to enroll his death, it grieves my heart and gives me more pain and grief to give you an account of the sadness of the occurrence. On arriving at this place yesterday evening Sam was sitting out on the platform between two boxes of the train [we] came in on, when the bolt that held them together broke suddenly and he fell in between the cars and the wheels run over him and killed him almost instantly. He was not able to speak but a very few words. He said that he would not be able to reach home any more. He requested his friends to ease his pain and they gave him cloriform that lulled his pain and he died in a few moments. I did not see the sad occurrence as I was a few boxes ahead of him. I never had the opportunity of seeing him until after he died, but I assure you he did not die without the grief of his company and friends for he was highly respected by those that knew him, and his loss is mourned by over a great many of the Arkansaw volunteers and all respect and honour that is necessary will be paid to him. Although he is far from home and in a strangers land, he is not here without friends to mourn his loss, Father Mother Brother Sisters and friends do not mourn over his loss for sooner or later we must all die, and us try to be prepared to meet around Gods holy this one that is gone. Friends pray for me and pray for the time is very precious. I must bring the sad account of my friends death to a close. Our regiment is now regularly formed and all of the companies constituting our regiment are now encamped, Albert Rust is our Colonel, a man by the name of Barton is Lutenant, Colonel V. H. Manning is Major. Dr. Wright, Sergeon, Dr. Pursley his assistant, Holoway quarter master and store comisary and parson Madison Chapel. We left Lynchburg yesterday morning and arrived at this place late yesterday evening. We expect to leave this place this evening to meet the enemy. We have to go on foot we don't know how far we will have to march on foot for we don't know how soon we may meet the enemy. We are now encamped in the valley where General George Washington was encamped and the land he watched over in darkest hours of the revolution. Friends I could write a lengthly letter but I have but a few moments more to write as our company is in commotion so I must bid you a dew this the last time that I will have the opportunity to write to you for a while and perhaps forever. Pray for me and let us try to meet in heaven deare friends and relatives. I must come to a close I would like to write you a lengthly letter but I must come to a close and trust God for the future. Do not write until you hear from us again although I havent received a letter from home since I left. Isac and my self are in good health at the present time. Fare well deare friends fare well give my respects to all my friends and relatives.

Yours truly
Nicholas C. Denson
I remain your affectionate son N. C. Denson

*A*s my company did not get first position of Company A in the organization of the Regiment, Capt Wilkins took Company K. Our first camp was on Alleghaney Mountain, second at Crab Valley between the mountain and Greenbrier River, where we camped for some two months. In September we went on two expeditions led by Col. Rust over mountains and along rivers with roads, trying to dislodge the enemy on Cheat Mountain. We fought our first battle at Greenbrier River October 3, 1861. The attacking general, Renele Ted, failed. We remained at Greenbrier River until November 22, when we broke camp and marched to Stratsburg and thence to Winchester where we wintered, save when we went on an expedition to Bath and Remeny, that's 40 miles west of Winchester, under command of General Stonewall Jackson.

Early in the spring of '62, we went to Soldsburro, N.C., and remained until just before the Seven Days Battle around Richmond. Here we were in Walkers Brigade, Homes Division. We were under fire of the enemy's gun boats but not actively engaged, but I stood as special picket the night McClennon fell back to City Point. After which we done picket duty at Chester, the halfway station between Richmond and Petersburg. After which we took up our tedious march to Maryland. We crossed and recrossed the Potomac, and on the 17th of Sept. 1862 at Sharpsburg or Antetium, our first bloody battle. My Company K lost eight killed, and about twice that number wounded.

Six of the killed were my mess mates. James Hughes, my first wife's oldest brother; Isaac Denson, my cousin;

Reynolds and Hammock; Pat Davis; and Nichols; and W. M. Stinson, my bed mate, was wounded. E. L. Bingham and myself out of the nine that went into battle were unhurt. It was a great slaughter of dear boys.

We slept on the battle field that night among the dead and dying. The night of the 18th, we recrossed the Potomac. P.S.: Just before we crossed to Maryland to the Sharpsburg Battle, we went to Harpers Ferry by force march. We were part of the troops that surrounded and captured about 14 or 15 thousand of the enemy. After this battle, it was a sad time with me when I sat down to write the sad news to loved ones at home.

Those of us left had little time to muse over the past, but we dropped a silent tear for loved ones who slept their last sleep. We believed our cause to be just. We went forward trusting in God, determined to do our duty as we now saw it. The enemy now having failed to capture Richmond by way of City Point or by the Sharpsburg Mount changed commanders and placed Joe Hooper in command and attempted to cross the Rappihannock River at Frederickburg. About the 10th of December 1862 by force marching, we commenced to mass our men to meet their advance. By our faithful men under James Longstreet on the right and Stonewall Jackson on the left, we drove them back across the Rappihannock, and Lincoln changed commanders, and Burnside was placed in command.

After a hard cold winter trying by different routes to accomplish that cherished hope in Dec. at Fredericksburg,

Va., my regiment The Third Arkansas, Col. Manning, Lieut. Col. Taylor, Maj Reedy, was placed in a brigade with the 1st, 4th, and 5th Texas regiments and through the balance of the war as the Texas Brigade, Hoods Division, Longstreet Corps of the Army of Northern Virginia.

In the first part of the spring of 1863, we were sent to Suffolk. In the meantime, Grant was put in command with his gun boats and Army. He strove to drive away and divide the Confederacy by taking and keeping possession of the Miss. River, so Lee started a campaign in early summer. I, with others, was willing to go whither-so-ever Lee said and led. We marched through Northern Virginia, crossed in Maryland thence into Pennsylvania on to Gettysburg, where, on the first of July our forces met the enemy west of Gettysburg and drove them back to the town and Little Round Top where on the 2nd my command engaged the enemy at two o'clock p.m. and fought until night fall, held the field, slept on our arms that night after the hardest evening's fight of the war. I visited this battle field after 50 years and located the ground which is still woods and in sight.

An incident occurred here on the 2nd just before we went into battle. I was one of the color guard with the flag. My position in the front rank on the right of the colors. I prided in position, but Capt J. W. Wilkins went to Col. Van H. Manning and said, "Col., we are going into battle today, and I want all of my non-commissioned officers with the company. Send Denson to the Company." Which order was given and obeyed. After that evening's battle, the color bearer and one color guard were all that were left that were not killed or wounded. Not only a hard one but one of the bloodiest battles of the war. On the 3rd we were under fire all day but not actively engaged in line of battle at the foot of the Little Round Top while several hundred pieces of artillery on Cemetery Ridge opened up on the camp of the enemy on top of Round Top just before Picket made his celebrated charge.

After that charge, we marched back to Cemetery Ridge, two or three hundred yards in our rear, where we spent that night on our arms. We spent the 4th of July on the field hoping that the enemy would come, but they did not. At nightfall of the 4th, we marched to Hagerstown, Maryland, where we stayed until the night of the 11th when we marched back towards Virginia and recrossed the Potomac River into Virginia.

On the morning of the 12th, we were in Northern Virginia, drilling, resting, and recruiting until the early part of September when we received orders for Longstreet Corp composed of McClellen's and Hood's Division to go to the Western Bragg Army down in Georgia. So we marched to Petersburg, took the train through the Carolinas to Georgia. So on the 18th got off the train and marched through the heat and dust towards Chickamauga, where the forces of Bragg and Rosencranze were in battle. Again, the morning of Saturday, the 19th of Sept., my Captain asked the Col. to send me back from the flag to the Company. That evening we attacked the enemy who ambushed my command, killed Major Reedy, and killed and wounded a number of our brave boys, but those of us left raised the Rebel Yell and drove them before us.

That evening while resting on our arms, I learned through Sergt. Major Hyatt that J. V. Williams, a mess mate and bed mate, was lying severely wounded in the head, so John Hill, another comrade, and I went and bore him to the rear to a place of safety. We slept on our arms that night on the battle field. The next morning, Sunday morning, the 20th, just as day was dawning, Harlston, the Company messenger boy, or courier, came to me in line, woke me up, and said, "Col Manning says for you to report to him." He was lying in line at the head of the regiment. I reported and said, "Col. I'm here." He said, "Denson, go to the rear, look up the wagon train, tell Bob Rust, Commissary Clerk, to bring my meat wagon for my men to have something to eat." I obeyed orders by taking my gun and went to the rear.

At least a mile or more back across Chickamauga Creek, found wagon and Rust, delivered my message, and hurried back to the regiment, which I found getting into line for an advance. We were soon in the charge. I had my gun broke at the lock by a minie ball. The gun was broke, but it saved my body as I was in the act of tapping my gun which I had just fired at the enemy who were charging. We routed the enemy. Our colors fell several times. Saturday the 19th and Sunday the 20th my Col. at this point presented me with the colors.

I have been on this battle field twice since the war. Here is where Gen. John D. Hood lost a leg. After this battle we were encamped at Chattanooga for sometime. I did some scouting with scouts by permission of Col. Manning and my Captain. I went with 11 others across Lookout Mountain on to what is known now as Sand Mountain, spent a day and night, and on the second day, which was Sunday, had a thrilling experience as we, 12 in number, attacked a scouting party of the enemy, killed one, captured 13, and brought them safe into camp. After this my command was moved to the west side of Lookout Mtn. for a few days where we had a skirmish with the enemy.

Early in December Longstreet Corp was ordered to Knoxville, Tennessee, which place we surrounded and would have forced them to surrender had not Gen Bragg lost at Chicamauga and Missionary Ridge. We marched from Knoxville further east, spent the winter of '63 and '64 in and around Morristown and Sweetwater, east Tennessee. This was one of the coldest winters of the war. About April of '64 took up our march back to Virginia and after a tiresome and weary march, footsore and ragged, we were welcomed by the noble ladies of Charlottsville, Virginia, Jefferson's old home town. Here we got new clothing which was much needed. We changed brigade commanders, General Roberson, familiarly known and called by the boys of the Texas Brigade "Old Billy," was relieved of the command of the Brigade, and Gen. Judge Grooe, of Texas, was placed in command of the brigade.

We commenced to drill and get ready for the spring campaign. Gen. U. S. Grant was made the commander of the Federal Forces. Our much beloved Robert E. Lee was in command of the Confederates of Northern Virginia. The armies of the two generals met in the country known as the Wilderness on the 4th and 5th of May. On the 5th of May the battle was severe. My Longstreets Corps was many miles away at Gordonsville but by force march the night of the 5th we arrived on the battle field just as two divisions of our best troops were surprised in the early morning of the 6th and almost routed.

Just as my brigade, the Texas, and the Bennings Georgia Brigade came marching up on the plank road. Here is where Gen Lee attempted to lead the Texas Brigade into battle. The brave boys cried, "Lee to the rear, and we go to the front." Then Cap. Harding of the 1st Texas Regiment led Lee's horse to the rear, and we did go to the front and force the enemy back but we lost more than half of our brave boys, killed and wounded. We went in, that is, my, the 3rd Arkansas Regiment, with 17 officers and came out with five and men lost in proportion. Col. Manning wounded, Lieut. Col. Taylor wounded, and my beloved Capt. J. W. Wilkins, now major, was killed. His last words to me after the first charge, "Denson, I'm glad to see you here." The next charge, which was soon, he was killed.

That day was a sad day for us when our lines had been advanced and we were arranging to drive Grant. Gen. Longstreet, Gen. Jenkins, of S. Carolina, with some of their staff were reconnoitering when our own men mistook them for the enemy and fired on them, killing Gen. Jenkins, brigadier general, and severely wounding Lieut. Gen. Longstreet. This caused us to check and halt for the evening. At night we held the field and slept on our arms. On the 7th, 8th, and 9th, Grant, failing to break through our lines kept moving towards Spotsylvania Court House where on the 10th another bloody battle. But Grant failed to break through our lines. Late in the evening of the 10th the enemy assaulted my brigade, crying No Quarter, they were repulsed with great loss but I was wounded in the ear and head and had to go to the rear to hospital where I was for 40 days. Tho I was not able for duty, I asked the doctor to let me join my regiment which I did in the ditches of Petersburg.

Later were ordered to the north side of James River. We were in several skirmishes, and on the 7th of October we fought a bloody battle. General Gregg was killed, and I went under the shots of fire seeming the worst I was ever under, back to the remnant of my regiment. Leaving a number of my comrades who were taken prisoners. In the number was Cap. Gill Martin who commanded the right wing of the regiment and I was Orderly Sergt. for his division. Just before this battle seven or eight miles out from Richmond, we were attacked by Negroes. Those of them that were not killed were repulsed and driven back but that day we were attacked by an overwhelming number 25,000 against 2500. We held them all day until late in the evening we got some reinforcements. From this time on there was more or less fighting.

Grant tried to break through our lines to Richmond and Petersburg but he failed, but what he could not do by assault he succeeded in doing as he had so many more men than we. He moved south toward Weldon, N.C. and tapped the railroad leaving us only one railroad south, so on the 2nd of April we left Richmond marching toward Appomattox Court House, fighting in the day and marching at night.

On the morning of the 9th of April, Lee found Gen. Thomas had come in on his front and Grant in our rear. His calvary on the flanks thus surrounded, our beloved commander Robert E. Lee, as I believe the greatest general of the continent, surrendered us that day. He said, I heard him, "Men, I have surrendered you, and you will be permitted to return home and remain unmolested until exchanged, and if ever exchanged I am ready and willing to lead you again."

My regiment at the surrender was commanded by Capt A. C. Jones of company 8, whose home was, and still is, at Three Creeks, in Union County, Arkansas. He is still living. He is the first man that ever called on me for public prayer. In 1864 about August, eight miles east of Richmond where we fought Negroes, my company K was commanded by Capt J. W. Morris. I was Orderly Sergt. T.P. Brewer signed my parole, which I still have. Capt. Jones said to the boys of the Regiment, 3rd Arkansas, "You can remain together under my command and we will go back to

Richmond and down the James to Fortress Monroe around New Orleans and thence up the Mississippi River and out to your several homes, or go at will on your own motion. I chose to be my own general and boss, so the morning of the 13th of April, 1865, more than a thousand miles from home and loved ones, without money or rations, in company with one comrade, William M. Bell of Mississippi, we bid farewell to Appomattox Court House and the boys of '61 to '65 and took up our line of march for Danville, Va., ninety miles away, which we reached the third evening just in time to be too late to catch a train for Greensboro, N.C. where we passed Johnson's army that surrendered on the 26th of April at Charlotte, N.C.

We passed Pres. Davis and ex-governor Lubbock of Texas, who was with Davis, here in person. Davis, at the request of Lubbock, examined my parole. The first and perhaps the last one from the army of Northern Virginia. We rode when we could and walked when we couldn't ride and somewhere in Georgia fell in company with Jim Trip of 18th Mississippi Regiment. He was alive a few years ago in Hinds County, Miss. We three rode from Atlanta, Georgia, on the train to West Point, Ga., where we crossed the river, held a council of war, walked 87 miles to Montgomery, Alabama, where we entered into the Federal lines. I had copied the terms of agreement between Grant and Lee, relative to transportation for paroled soldiers of the army of northern Virginia and had it with me. It said we should have transportation on Federal and Confederate transportation lines.

On our way here we reached Montgomery, Al, about twelve o'clock on the third day footsore and hungry. We left on the Federal transport down the Alabama River about sundown that evening and reached Selma, Al, before day the next morning. Learning the next morning that my beloved old Captain, J. W. Wilkins' wife and baby were living in Selma. I visited with them a few minutes. I talked with his sad hearted widow. When I got back to Bell and Trip they were in company with Cousins of Alabama, who was on Gen. E. M. Law's staff at the Battle of Gettsyburg and on the evening of the 3rd of July after Picket's charge, came to my command at the foot of Little Round Top and piloted us out into the open and told us we were ordered to form on and hold Cemetery Ridge.

He, Cousins, accompanied Bell, Trip and myself to the town limits of Selma, Al, and bid us farewell. I met him some 30 years afterwards at Houston, Texas at a reunion of soldiers. I recognized him and spoke to him. From Selma we made forced march, ten miles, caught a train for Dempolis, took boat for seven miles on the Tombigbee River, connected with a train at Meridian, Miss., slept on the train at night. Gen. Dick Taylor's command of Confederates was at Meridian when we passed. They surrendered on May 6. Bell and I got off at Horton, Miss. and walked 19 miles to his home at Good Hope, Leak County, Miss.

Arriving there at night the 4th of May, having traveled a thousand miles riding some six hundred and walking the rest. I visited kinfolks in Leak County, Scott and Rankin

County, worked some in the wheat fields and on the morning of June 19, with a suit of new clean clothes, fifty cents in silver, in company with Bell, I left Uncle and Aunt and a very dear cousin, Helen Bell, and rode horseback to Horton, eighteen or nineteen miles, where Bell left me and I took a train for Jackson, Mississippi. Before Will Bell left me at Horton I said, "Bill, I wish I had one comrade with me." He said, "You won't go far before you meet some fool."

And when I went aboard the train a little after twelve o'clock, I met R. M. Roberts and B. F. Simpson of M Company and A. Boyd of Company D of my regiment and as they had no provision and did not try to get any at Vicksburg while I was trying to get transportation for four of us up the Miss. River on Harricon Deck to Gaines Landing, I had to divide my rations with them, and when we landed on the Arkansas side about one hour by sun the evening of June 21, we had one biscuit apiece.

The last day, the 22nd of June, I marched on foot fifty miles and met stepfather and Joe Baldy, a half brother, that evening. I met my very dear old mother who came on horseback. The next day I got into my home a little after dark the 23rd of June 1865. Met my brothers, N. Denson and Rufus Denson and Emiley Denson and Casandrie Denson, my two sisters and the Negroes I had left the 31st of May 1861. The next morning I went horseback three miles to Aunt Frankie Daniels near Fountain Hill. She lost two sons, W. W. Daniel at Sharpsburg, Sept. 17, 1862, and Jessie on the 7th of Oct., 1864, on the skirmish line east of Richmond, and as I had helped to bury Jessie in the Rockies in the edge of Richmond, I visited her to tell her about her boys.

After a short talk and stay with her I went next to the W. M. Hughes home, the father of my first beloved wife. Late in the evening that day I rode back home. As it was too late to start a crop and as all I had was a sound body, active mind, and burning desire to do something and be somebody, I commenced to cast about and consult with my oldest brother, N. E. Denson, what to do first. My oldest brother was a good sensible man, but health gone he was a physical wreck. My two sisters and younger brother must be cared for. I wanted to go to school but I could not as I had to work day and sometimes night for food while my sisters spun and wove clothes.

So I got a team of mules from a neighbor, R. L. Belcher putting my services against the team and started out with four mules and an old wagon that had the misfortune to break down nearly every trip. My first trip out with team and wagon, I started with twenty bushels of wheat to a wheat mill on Saline River thirty miles from Fountain Hill and four miles from Warren, owned by uncle Sam Turner. I got about four miles from home and stalled. Four big mules, twenty bushels of wheat had to be unloaded and reloaded by myself. I am glad I was a christian boy then, but I soon got those mules so when they started up a hill and I said "Hold" they kept pulling until they got to the top of the hill, so I could keep up a lively whistle. I am still a whistler when it goes well and I have nobody to talk to.

I saved enough money from my hard earnings of the latter part of '65 to assist in launching a crop with my oldest brother as partner and my younger brother as a helper on the farm with the promise from my older brother and myself to my youngest brother that he should go to school next year, 1867.

The Negroes all left about Christmas, 1865, and none but the whites, three brothers and two sisters as family. My oldest brother, N. E. Denson, my partner, was so impaired in health by Scrofula it was with great pain he worked. But the noble spirited boy he was, struggled on working by day and suffering at night. Negroes being free and my mother, by the mismanagement of my stepfather, P. H. Baldy, was left without a home of her own, and as brother and I had rented the Harris place on Flat Creek, two and a half miles north of our home, which had a house on it, we let mother and family of three small children, two boys, Edward and Joe, and one girl with Stephfather, P. H. Baldy, when at home, occupy the house. So brother and I worked in the field and sisters kept house at home while mother kept house with her children and worked day and parts of night.

Brother and I in our poverty, by God's grace, with zeal and determination did our best and succeeded in supplying food for all. While we cultivated the crop on the last day of May we had a fine prospect for a crop and were happy and cheerful as could be under the circumstances.

But on the night of June 1, there came a storm of wind, rain and hail that caused stout hearts to almost doubt. The morning of the 2nd of June being Saturday when we looked out on the home on the creek as brother Luther and I spent the night at mothers, so we could go to work early in the morning, to our sorrow and dismay when we looked out, the water was running over the drop from two to five feet deep. So early in the morning, on foot, brother Luther and I started for our little home two and a half miles south, where our oldest brother, Norfleet had gone the night before to stay with sisters, having carried the plows with him calculating to commence to lay by nine acres of nice hill corn.

Monday morning when brother Luther and I got in about a mile of our home and saw some trees uprooted by the wind and storm, I said to brother, "There has been a storm here." We walked on and soon met older brother coming riding a mule. He called and said "Are all alive?" We answered, "Yes, but the water over the crop." He said, "The wind and hail has wrecked our home and destroyed the crop." Every house and cabin on the place save the dwelling was unroofed or partly so, but when brother Luther and I reached home, after greeting sisters and looking around a few minutes, we started straightening up and rebuilding wrecked houses and fences. We worked until just before sundown.

I said to brother Luther, who was my partner in the repair work, "Let's go up to the house and clean up our persons, put on the best clothes we have and start out, one go east and the other west." I went about a half a mile to my nearest neighbors house, Mr. McPhail. The old man was away from home and the water on the creek so high he could not get home for several hours. His two girls, fine portly looking young ladies, had been working all day as Brother and I had, making repairs and trying to save what was left. So we struggled on and made a fair crop but my oldest brother who had worked in pain by day and doctored and suffered by night, after the crop was layed by, had to give up and commence to think about going to New Orleans to Dr. Stone for treatment.

A neighbor by the name of C. P. Lowery undertook to raise money to defray his expenses and was succeeding nicely, but my noble hearted brother gave the money back with thanks and said, "I will wait." And in October younger brother and I got out two bales of cotton and it ginned, put it on a wagon, and my oldest brother and I left for a point of the Miss. River 50 miles where we shipped it to Hawthorne and Martin through Capt. Gill Martin of war fame, who when he saw me 50 yards away said, "Old fellow, if I had known once what I know now I would have gone, too." That cotton sold for 36-and-a-half cents a pound, and we paid the government three cents a pound revenue which was unconstitutional, which money they are still due me and ought to pay.

We bought flour at $14.50 a barrel, half a barrel of sugar, 15 lbs of coffee, got $75.00 in money and commenced arranging on our return home to get older brother off to New Orleans to Dr. Stone. Later in November, I went back to Unice on horseback and got the balance of the returns on the cotton, $86.00, as well as I remember. I think I ought to stop here and give another bit of history that affected my life very materially.

I wanted to go to school and prepare myself for life's very battle. I thought it over and prayed over it. I felt it to be my duty to take care of my sisters and keep the promise brother and I had made to our younger brother to send him to school next year, which I did. But now, Oldest Brother was disabled by disease, and I, by God's loving providence, was left to work and grapple with problems, and as I decided at Appomattox in April '65 to trust God and go ahead, I prayed and decided the best thing for me to do was to marry. I knew who in heart I loved best but I had never told her so.

She did not live more than two and a half miles away but I sat down and wrote the true sentiments of my heart, telling her if it was reciprocated to answer. If not, to return my letter and we would still be friends. I sent that letter by hand and looked and hoped for the reply, or the return letter. It never came so finally a stout heart had to yield and so on Saturday night of the 18th of August, 1866, after preaching at Flat Creek Church, I asked Miss Rebecca Hughes if I could have the honor and pleasure of her company home. She granted the request, oh, fated night never to be forgotten. I told her I loved her and had loved her for years and asked her if she could love me. She said, "I think so." But I grow bold as we walked in the moonlight. "Do you love me?" In her modest, reserved way, she said, "Yes." I said, "Will you be mine for life?" She said,

"Yes." Then I said, "I have nothing but a heart to love and a hand to protect, to offer. If you will accept they will be yours." She accepted and I said, "Now let us keep this secret and don't listen to gossip or reports from others and if anything comes to your ears or mine let us not believe it until we see each other." Though it was two-and-a-half miles from her pa's home and mine and this was August the 18th and we did not marry until December 27, I visited her but twice in her home and she kept it secret.

❧

In November after Brother Luther and I had gathered most of the crop and I had to go into co-partnership with R. L. Belcher, hire three Negroes, and farm in 1867, I went with my brother, N. E. Denson, to Mary Salino, 28 miles on the Ouchita River in a buggy. We spent the night together in the old warehouse, a stormy night on the bank of the Ouachita River, the water all around us. He took the boat the next day for New Orleans hoping to be benefited by Dr. Stone's treatment. I bid him farewell next morning and hitched the mule to the borrowed buggy. The buggy belonged to Mr. Hughes, my anticipated father-in-law. The mule belonged to my future partner, Mr. Belcher. I started for home. The rains had caused the creeks to rise to overflowing and but few bridges were left when about 12 miles from home, I drove into a creek that was swimming and very swift. When about the middle, I saw my mistake and tried to free my mule and buggy upstream but was forced downstream by that strong current, and soon mule and buggy went under a large log across the stream. As the mule and buggy went under the log, I made a leap and landed on top of the log. Got to my feet just as the mule rose on the lower side of the log. Without taking time to hardly think, I pulled off my coat and plunged in, boots and clothing minus the coat left on top of the log. I swam to the mule, which had struck bottom in the bend of the creek. I took hold of the cheek of the bridle on the mule, took my knife out of my pocket with the other hand, cut the belly band and hamstring, loosed the lines, led the mule out of the overflow back on the side from hence I entered, leaving the buggy and harness in midstream. I hitched the mule to the corner of a fence nearby and started back up the road towards Judge Jim Pugh's in a trot.

I soon found out I needed dry clothes, as the wind was blowing a gale from the north as it had begun to fair off that November evening. I stopped at a country store belonging to J. D. Pugh, an army comrade, and run by his brother Dan Pugh, and Dan gave me some of John's old clothes that were in the store to put on while mine hung out to dry in the sunshine. I had a few dollars in greenbacks in my pocket. We dried that, and in company with Judge Pugh and Dan, we went back and got the mule. They took me in and lodged me for the night. The next morning Judge Pugh went with me and helped me to get my buggy out, mend my harness, and started me on my journey, rejoicing.

I went by where Miss Becky lived, left the buggy, and rode the mule on home though a day late. Miss Becky told me later of her anxiety that day. Well, as agreed on, my Miss Becky Hughes and I on the night of December 27th were married. We were to have an infair dinner the next day at my home, but that night Joseph Guice, a Negro boy of that neighborhood, stole Jin the mule, saddle, and bridle, and left for other parts. About an hour by the sun the next morning when my half-brother Ed Baldy, who was to bring horse and mule for Miss Becky and I to ride home and eat infair dinner, he came with horse minus the mule and my suspicion was aroused. I said to Miss. Becky, "You stay here at your pa's, and I will go in search for the mule."

After riding several hours and several miles, I got on a hot trail about 12 miles from home, about 10 miles south of Monticello. I went on until within four miles of Monticello, I saw with bridle and saddle hitched to palings in front of Brother R. Y. Royal's house, the Negro standing between the house and the gate. He, the Negro, was in the act of trading the mule to Mr. Greenlee for a horse and $20.00 to boot, so I took charge of the Negro and mule, and in order to make the Negro secure, I tied his arms so they would hang limp by his sides and put him on my horse, and I rode the mule, which had a good saddle, a better saddle than the horse and, as I desired to, got back where Miss Becky was as early as possible.

I let the Negro ride instead of making him walk. It was very cold. The sun shone until just before sunset, when it clouded up and began to sleet and snow. I went by Mr. Benson's to see his son Porter, who had gone to Longview, 10 miles on the Saline River, to look for the mule, and to let him know I had the mule and thief and was going back to my wife's house. I was riding head up and in good spirits. It was now night and snow falling fast, just north of Fountain Hill and two miles from Mr. Hughes. I looked around, and to my surprise and dismay old John, the horse the Negro was riding, was pacing along without a rider. Just before that moment was the last time I ever saw John Guice, though I hunted that night and the next morning with dogs and double-barrel shotgun.

So the next morning Miss Becky and I rode home through a blinding snow storm to start life together. I ate my first meal at home about three P.M. On the 29th of December 1867. After a few days' stay at home, I left sister Casandrie and Emiley and brother R. L. Denson on the little home, my brother being in New Orleans, and took my wife some two miles north to the farm where the Negroes were. That was an eventful year filled with thrilling and eventful experiences. About the first of March, my brother came home to die. Oh how we did love him and how he did love us.

∞

My dear young wife and I with the Negroes went to the home place to work the 13th day of March and planted some corn, but in the afternoon it clouded up and began to snow. I had the Negroes to load the wagon with corn and start for the other farm, and I lingered behind to talk with my brother. A runner came and said the wagon load of corn had bogged down. I bid my dear brother goodby and went to the assistance of the Negroes. I went on home to where my dear wife was. Just one week from that day, March 20, my mother's birthday, a runner, or messenger, came and said, "Come quickly, your brother can't live long." I went post haste to him, my wife to come later on horseback, but when I reached him his spirit had gone to God who gave it.

I strove on through trials and difficulties and poverty with my precious wife, a great deal of the time sick, but never murmured or complained, and made a crop and came out in debt, moved back to my little home, let the Negroes go who owed me for provision more than I owed. I gave my sisters and brother all that belonged to my older brother. Our first babe, Helen Hughes Denson, was born September 25. So early in 1868, wife, babe, and I moved back home in the house with sisters and brother, but soon my youngest sister, Emiley, sickened and died.

Soon afterwards, Stepfather died and left Mother and three children, half-brothers and sisters. I did the best thing under the circumstances. I took them to my house and shared roof and bread with them. Three families under one roof, and if there was ever a hard feeling between my dear old mother and sweet precious wife, I never knew it. My brother and I made a good crop that year and got a good price for it. The next year I got a house for Mother and children, furnished team. Her boys and Brother and I worked through, though we had separate crops. The next year being '70, I got the home for her. Brother and Sister lived with them. They made a good crop and got a good price and were self sustained. But it was a sad year for my dear wife and I who were alone in the home and at first, oh, so happy, but in July just as I got a buggy so we could go together, sweet little Carrie Bell Denson, who was born August 28, 1869, took sick with cholera infantum and after a week's suffering on the 21st of July died.

Then again in October, our dear three year old, Helen Denson, on the 18th of October died, and as we walked from the graveyard, my dear wife leaning on my arm, how sad we were. When we reached our home, childless, the first thing we did was to kneel down and pray to our God and Father. Next February 2, 1871, our dear boy W. A. Denson was born, which brought new life and care to our hearts and home. The years '71, '72, and '73 were spent on our little farm west of Fountain Prairie. On June 1, 1873, another baby girl was born: Emma Bradford Denson. In the fall of '73, I sold the little farm to Richard Lock on credit and moved to W. M. Stinson's farm four miles northwest near the county line between Ashley and Drew. I farmed in 1874 with W. M. Stinson, helping to repair fences for rent. That was a very dry year and a short crop that fall.

Mr. Stinson married Miss Till Dean and they lived in '75 with her parents in Bare House. I rented Stinson's farm.

My wife's youngest brother, Matt M. Hughes, a good boy, worked with me. We made a good crop.

That winter I moved to my father-in-law's place, one-and-one-half miles south of Fountain Hill, as Father-in-law moved with his family to the Mississippi River at Luna Landing. I made repairs on the place for rent in 1876. In 1875 Flat Creek Church, my old church, licensed me to preach and made appointment for me to preach, but oh, how it did rain that night, so I did not preach that night. We made another appointment, and I preached my first sermon at Flat Creek Church in 1876.

My text, "Who Hath Believed Our Report," Isiah 53:1. The year of 1876 was election year, and I was Central Committeeman from White Township. I made a good crop that year and made some collections on the place sold to Lock, but not enough to get away to Texas, so I went in the latter part of the summer to Bradley County, and as my wife had one sister, Mary E. Mack, whom she loved very dearly, living in Warren, I spent the night in her home and talked to her and her husband, W. F. Mack, relative to future plans and agreed to move on the tract of land bought by him, Mack, from Hale.

I bought half interest in said place located two-and-a-half miles southwest of Warren on the Middle Moro Road. Moved on the place in November 1876 and made my first crop in Bradley County in 1877, assisted by John Lock and Ben Rice, white boys, and paid them wages. We made a good crop, but my, how we did work. That year I preached a few sermons as a licensated, and in the meantime I had joined with my wife in the Warren Baptist Church. Bro. W. Y. Moran was the preacher. He was a great preacher. He advised me to wait until some church called for my ordination before I accepted ordination, which I did.

W. E. Paste, a great man and preacher, followed Moran in the pastorate of the Warren Church. In May 1878 M. L. Gardner visited me and told me that Smyrna Church, situated in the southern part of Bradley County, wanted me to preach for them. Just before this time, Lucy Hughes Denson was born, April 11, 1878, so now I had a wife tried and true and three children depending on me for support. I was poor in this world's good, limited in education and Bible knowledge, and a burden on my head, woe unto me if I preach not the gospel. In '75, my mother, who was a great Bible student, died. In '76, my sister Casandrie Denson Bull died leaving one little girl, Lena Bull Sneed.

Soon through J. B. Searcy's influence, Enon Church of Cleveland County across the river from Warren called me to preach for them. Smyrna, by resolution in conference, asked the Warren Baptist Church to set me apart to the full gospel ministers, consisting of M. Y. Morgan, J. B. Searcy, Solomon Gardner, and W. E. Paxton, the pastor, to meet at the Baptist Church in Warren on the Sunday (1st) In September 1878 to ordain N. C. Denson to the full work of the ministery. So when morning came and I arrived, W. E. Paxton and Solomon Gardner, with the church and all members of the council invited, present, they organized and proceeded with the examination and ordination. Just here I think is the place to record that J. H. Riggin, a Methodist minister who was at my mother's bedside just before she went home to glory and heard her say to me, "Son, if you feel you have a work to do, don't resist," he, Riggin, was at the ordination service.

I was soon preaching every Sunday and working six days on the farm during the week. I kept this up about 15 years, in the meantime building me a comfortable home one-and-three-fourth's miles southwest of Warren, where my family and I lived happy. Here, one day I saw my dear wife standing by my bedside, weeping, and I said, "I knew it would come to this someday, but I didn't think so quick." I was sick in bed, not boasting, but because it was true. Permit me to say for 40 years through God's goodness to me, I had not been in bed a week at a time, so by His Grace I was soon up and going.

One day I said, "Wife, I am going to quit working free Negroes." She said, "I will believe it when I see it." I said, "If you live, you will see it." Again one day I said, "Wife, I'm going to quit raising cotton." She said, "I will believe it when I see it." I said, "If you live, you will see it." Here, I left my three children all in bed with measles and rode horseback 25 miles and preached, leaving no one but my dear beloved, consecrated wife with them, and God, who I served in my spirit and body, knows I love them all.

After preaching Saturday, I went home with W. H. Barringer, ate supper, and he and I rode five miles to see

Bro. J. C. Gillis, who was sick on his death bed. We spent the night. In the night he, Gillis, had his wife wake up and told her to get his pocketbook, a large leather pocketbook he kept notes and papers in. He took from it a note against J. E. Meek with J.R.S. Meek as security, for $665.00, put it under his pillow and said to me, "Make me remember in the morning what I am talking about tonight." So the next morning, I, at the suggestion of Murphy, his step-son-in-law who was present that night, spoke to his wife about it. So she said, "Mr. Gillis, do you want me to give Bro. Denson that note?" He said, "No, give it to me." He took it and sat up in bed and put the other hand on my head, in the presence of his wife and God to witness, and said, "You have been the best friend I have ever had." I said, Bro. Gillis, I fear you appreciate me too much. He said, "Not to you, but to the Lord."

He was the grandfather of Mrs. Mollie Herring, who with his wife heired the estate. I got every dollar of that $665.00, and my house in Warren is the fruit of it. I bade him goodbye that morning, never saw him any more as he died eight days later. I never knew it until he was dead and buried. I went from his house that morning, Sunday, to Concord Church, where his membership was, and preached. Got dinner on the way. Went five miles to Union Hall Church, preached at three o'clock P.M., rode home arriving about 9 P.M. tired in body and mind. Met my beloved partner and consecrated wife watching with those dear children whom God cared for in my absence and permitted me to find improving. Oh my, the goodness and mercy of my God and Father, blessed be His name forever.

About this time, the Bartholomew Association met at Lake Village. Bro. Solomon Gardner and I went through the country in a buggy, he furnishing the buggy and me the horses, from Warren to Lake Village. It was while at Lake Village at the meeting I heard Bro. J. S. Woods say as the letters from churches were being read, "See, he baptized more than all of us." I served one church, Ebenezer, five-and-one-half miles west of Warren, 12 years without intermission. I was pastor at Warren twice, first for six years and then in mission work three years. Then by earnest request of the Warren Church, I served them five years more, making in all 11 years, for half time. During this time, I was elected moderator of my Bartholomew Association and then without intermission for eight years or nine, I was moderator.

I have served since that time, twice I think, as moderator. I was 20 odd years on the State Mission Board. Elected in January 1897 Chaplain of the Arkansas House of Representatives. Served four months again in 1905. Then again in 1905 was elected State Chaplain of the Arkansas State Senate, served four months, kept up my work up and down the Iron Mountain Railroad and missed only four roll calls in four months. I have a gold-headed cane as a token of their appreciation. I have been missionary of the Association for two years and the State Board a number of years.

Organized the Wilmar Church and saw building built. Organized church at Crossett and a building erected. Organized a church at Dermott, done soliciting, planning, and having house built, and preached for them eight years. Organized churches at Montrose and McGehee, also Morrell. Reorganized church at Collins and helped organize Arkansas City and Blissville. Preached at Portland 11 years. Seven years the first time and saw a house built, then after four years went and preached four years more.

Have been twice vice-president of the Arkansas Baptist State Convention. Preached four years at Hamburg. Have preached for the last 38 years in southeast Arkansas, baptized hundreds, married hundreds of couples, and helped to bury great numbers. Hold two meetings in Texas and one in Mississippi, and though am now past 75 years of age, thanks be to God, am still active in his service.

After the death of my two sweet children in 1870, there was not a death in my family for 28 years. We raised three children to be grown and now married. In 1892, my beloved wife had a half-sister to die leaving two little orphan boys, Leicoster, nearly five years old, and Dixie Hannibal, nearly three years old, without homes or visible means of support. We took them into the home April 11, 1892, and shared bread and shelter with them for 12 years. Both are still living and married. Leicoster Hannibal and wife in Los Angeles, California, and Dixie Hannibal and wife in Batesville, Arkansas, as railroad agent, and has been railroad agent with good salary since before he was 16 years of age.

I had a great desire to give my children better education advantages than I had. I sent Billie to Ouachita College one session, and he seemed to think that the world would come to an end without his gaining distinction if he didn't work. Billie is a grand boy, and the world about him knows he is living in it. He has a noble, true wife in the person of Fay Wilson Denson and two sweet precious boys, all the grandchildren I have of my own. The health of my precious wife, Rebecca Hughes Denson, began to fail some two or three years before the end came.

Early in January 1897 when I was elected Chaplain of the House of Representatives, I started Emma Denson Clements back to Ouachita. She went in 1896, and this was her second year in college. The next year we started baby girl, Lucy Denson Daniel. She entered Sept. 1897, and when she came home in June 1898, her mother, the idol of all our hearts, was failing rapidly in health. We all showed her every attention and kindness. How precious the memories of her, still, though 18 years have come and gone, but on the 13th of August 1898 about three P.M., one of the dearest and sweetest lives went out. "She rests from her labors, and her works do follow her." Sweet one, rest on. Someday we shall meet where parting will be no more.

So in September, Lucy went back to Ouachita, and Emma, the big girl with the big warm heart, kept house doing her best, and that was making home still dear and sweet to us all. Lucy wrote to me just before school closed her second year, saying, "Papa, if you don't object, I am going to contract with Prof Conger to go to school at Ouachita another year and finish my Elocution in Music and I will teach and pay it when I get home." We have a note for what was due at the end of the three years, and true to her promise, she got a class at Farmersville, La., and done her best, but what she failed to pay, the Lord enabled me to pay. So it was paid, and we got a cleared receipt.

She got home and learned her sister Emma was soon to be married to the man of her choice. A good man, take him around up and down, everyday, none better. I asked Lucy to go ahead and arrange to teach, and me and the boys would get along somehow, but she had a head like "Collins Sheep" and something like her Dad and with firmness of her mama, so she kept house, taught a little music, tried to keep in touch with the young folks, so home went on pretty smoothly.

So I began to think if I could find the right kind of a lady, it would be best for Lucy and me for me to marry the second time. I got my consent, but to find the right lady was a hard proposition. But after a while, I thought I had found one that would fill the bill. I made the venture, and about the time I thought I had made good, she said nothing doing. I thought and tried again, and this time she said yes, and stuck to it.

On the 28th day of July 1903, Mrs. Ellen Grubb and I met in Monticello at the Bussy Hotel and were married. That was 13 years ago last Friday, and I know I love her better today than I did 13 years ago. We know each other better. She is a noble true lady. Oh, I wish I could see her in good health again and could do more for her health and comfort in days to come than those that are gone. She had two children, Bruce Grubb a noble boy, and Maude Skippy, as fine as pure gold and worth a hundred cents on the dollar. I love to love Maude. Bruce and his wife have four children, one girl and three boys.

Maude and Charlie have one girl and one boy living and one boy dead. Vivian belongs to Grandma and Ben, and she is a premium. It would take more than gold to get her. I once thought my work was done, and I would live and die at Warren but 12 years gone last January 15, I moved to Dermott and began to grapple with new problems. I don't feel like I have been a failure as I have learned to live by the day. I work and pray to do my best every day, trusting God and trying to do good. I hope to be fed and live long on the earth. This is August 1916, and if I live and do well, I hope to write again some day.

Lucy, you and Scud can typewrite this and see I have not re-written or prepared before writing to write or desired to write history, but at the request of Lucy Daniel, my youngest daughter, to write a sketch of reminiscence of my life, especially that part pertaining to the War '61 to '65 and since without any written date to draw from. I have taken scraps from memories book and penned them as they came to me now after I have passed the 75 milepost. I am thankful to my kind Heavenly Father, who has been good to me and has given me memory that is still clear and active. A lady said a few days ago that W. J. Cone of

Montrose said, "If you want the pedigree of any man in Arkansas, especially in Southeast Arkansas, ask Bro. N. C. Denson." Now, after nearly a year has passed, July 24, 1917, and I am in the home alone, as Ellen, my beloved wife, is away at Eureka Springs with Vivian to try to get her health back, I will try to write again.

I am still active, preaching every Sunday and night, though I have passed my 76th birthday. Well, on Sept. 12, 1916, I left home on the early morning train, got to Little Rock at 10:30, went to the Mission Room, then to the Eighth Street Methodist Church to a temperance meeting. Left Little Rock at or after 5 P.M. for Batesville to visit Dick, Lena, and Claude Denson Hannibal. Arrived at Batesville after 9 P.M. Dick met me at Newport, spent eight days at Batesville, preached Sunday and night, visited the Masonic Orphans Home, the lock and dam on White River, the Batesville Stone Quary.

Had a good time and enjoyed my visit. This has been an eventful year as our beloved president has been forced to declare war against Germany, but I rejoice to see my country united, one flag standing behind the Christian president, determined indeed, to battle for the right. Through the kindness of friends, I attended the reunion of cc-confederate at Washington City, D.C. In June, saw the president. Had a great time. Visited Mt. Vernon, preached in Little Rock on my way going and coming. Preached the next morning and night at Parkdale. Visited the reunion at Vicksburg, Miss., in November.

Scud Daniel, Lucy's husband, had smallpox Christmas, and as I did not have to wait on him, as Lucy did that, I visited Billie's family, spent two nights and a day, spent one night with Brother and family at Fountain Hill, and then to Parkdale and Wilmot to preach.

It's 1918 and the war is still raging, and our beloved president, backed by Congress and a united people, is trusting God and doing our best to overcome wrong with right and might with right. A million soldiers in France and Europe and perhaps three million more under armies and encampments. This June 20th from May 15 to the 20th of June I attended the Southern Baptist Convention at Hot Springs, Arkansas, a great convention in numbers, 400, 220, in spiritual ability and brotherly love and accord. After working through July and a portion of August by day and night by advice of Dr. Hawkins of Markdale, I left the field in Arkansas and went to New Orleans and rested 10 days. The first rest after 41 years in the ministry.

Baptized a young lady the morning before I left for New Orleans, Sister Maude Cockrell at Parkdale, Arkansas. September 30, I left home for Bartholomew Association 10 miles north of Hamburg, spent the 1st and 2nd of October at the association. I preached the introductory sermon. Got back home 3 A.M. The 3rd, left for reunion of Ex-confederates at Atlanta, Ga., at 2 P.M. Spent Sunday the 5th at Little Rock. Arrived at Atlanta, Ga. with wife at 3 A.M. on the 7th. By 3:30 A.M., we were in bed in one of the best homes in Atlanta, Mr. Parsons, 618 Ponce DeLeon Street.

We spent the 7th, 8th, 9th, and 10th to the 12th and 13th in Atlanta, left for home, arrived at Dermott at 9 P.M. on the 11th, I changed clothing and went to Parkdale, 30 miles south of Dermott. Arrived at Parkdale at 3:30 A.M. in a downpour of rain. Slept about three hours and preached at 11 and at night. As it continued to rain, we both left Parkdale about 5 P.M. on the 15th for home. I arrived at Dermott about 7 P.M. I have been preaching Sunday and night since.

We had our Baptist Convention at Immanuel Church at Little Rock on the 12th and 13th. On the 16th I preached at Grady and spent two nights and a day with Emma and Dan. Preached three times on the 23rd. Spent Thanksgiving at Warren, spending two nights and one day with Billie and Fay and the three sweet children. Preached the fifth Sunday, November 30th, at McArthur. Preached twice, came home to Dermott where the church promised $9,000.00 for the 75 Million Campaign. I promised $250.00. So at 8 P.M., praising God and happy in His service, preached Friday night at Portland, Arkansas.

Before the 1st Sunday, Dec. 1st, at Wilmot, L. E. Barton met me and preached two sermons. The Wilmot Church agreed to pay $2,500.00 on the 75 Million Campaign for five years. Parkdale agreed to pay $2,600.00, and Blissville, by sister and brother J. P. Baker and children, $300.00. My wife went to bed sick Christmas morning. With many rememberances and gifts from loved ones, Christmas was not as pleasant as desired. Wife has been near death's door, but thankful to say she is much better this bright sunshiny morning, Jan 14, 1920.

∞

*A*fter more than four months, I write again, this May 27th, 1920. Wife, Ellen Harriet Denson, passed away January 23, 1920. "A precious one from us has gone, a voice we loved is still, a place is vacant in our home, which never can be filled." God in his wisdom has recalled by his love. The body slumbers here, the soul safe at rest. After the death of my beloved wife, I decided to let my mind have a chance for rest, and as February had five Sundays, I decided to go to the five. I was preaching and told them I must rest a while, and so, on the last day of March, I left for Mimbers, New Mexico, to visit three nieces, Jethro, Lena, and Mary Denson, my brother's girls.

I arrived at Mimbers the evening of the 3rd of April, remained until April 12, had a good time, preached once. I returned by the way of Oklahoma City, visited Cora Mack Peel, spent 24 hours, stopped in Little Rock, dined with B. P. and Bob Kidd. Spent a night at Grady with Dan and Emma Clements, reached and moved into my house, and am making home as pleasant as possible.

∞

*A*fter the death of my beloved wife, her daughter, Maude Skipper, lingered between life and death for six weeks, but has recovered and is in her new home. I left home May 8, spent two nights in Little Rock with Dixie, left the 10th for Washington, D.C., to attend the Southern Baptist Convention in numbers, 2,043. Work, spirituality, one million dollars for foreign missions, all debts paid, and more than $100,000 in the bank. A half million for home mission, all debts paid, money in the bank.

Brother and Sister Bottoms of Texarkana gave $100 each for foreign and home missions, many conversions, and baptisms. A great convention of great men and women, trusting in God with a mind to work and deny themselves. I saw God's spirit of power and love. Writing this June 20th at home alone, though past 77, I hope to yet be able and pray to do something to honor Him that has so wonderfully blessed me.

P. H. Baldy, my stepfather, died last Nov. 1, I believe. From September 24, 1918, to December 1, 1919, was the most eventful period of my life. Went with Chas A. Adkins to reunion of ex-confederate soldiers and had a great time. Returned to home at Dermott, Arkansas, for Bartholomew Association Oct. 5 to 7. C. R. Adkins was a guest at my home, had a great association. The night of the 7th a phone message from Dr. W. P. Baker to tell Uncle Nick that Dr. Cobb is dying. When I reached his bedside 34 miles away at Wilmot, he was dead. He, Cobb, had contributed to my expenses to Tulsa, Oklahoma. We buried him on the evening of Oct. 8. By the 10th, there was someone with influenza in almost every home in Wilmot. On the fourth Sunday in November, I was called home to help bury Harry Courtney, who died with flu in Dermott. Clark Sims, my beloved pastor, was stricken with flu on Saturday night before the fourth Sunday.

The mill at Blissville closed down for Thanksgiving services November 26. I held the service and came home to Dermott in the evening and took part in Thanksgiving service at night. Sims was very sick. On the 11th of November, the Armistice was signed. On Saturday before the first Sunday in 1918, I was called from Wilmot to Dermott as Clark Sims, beloved pastor had died 9:30 o'clock. We held services at Dermott Church Sunday evening about sundown. We left with the remains for Malvern, Arkansas at three A.M. Monday morning and arrived at Malvern via Little Rock, accompanied by his father, mother, and two brothers, Grady and Van and Van's wife and Henry Gaster, his brother-in-law, and others, where we buried him after holding services over his remains in a church he took a leading part in building when he was pastor at Malvern.

On Monday the 23rd, before Christmas, I was called to go to Wilmar to help bury Neal Barker. We buried him on the morning of the 24th at the chapel near his old home. I arrived at home in Dermott 9:30 P.M. On the 25th, Christmas Day. I married at 11 A.M. Charlie Measel and Miss Doll Anderson. Left that P.M. for my son's at Warren, accompanied by Lucy and Scud. Spent two nights and one day there in Warren.

On the morning of the 27th was called by phone to go to Montrose, Arkansas, as my beloved brother and comrade had died suddenly. We buried him that night and on the fifth Sunday in March 1918, we had memorial services at Fellowship Church at Snyder. In June 1919, my wife and Vivian went to Eureka Springs where they spent three-and-a-half months. Learning from Vivian that my wife was sick, I left home on Tuesday morning at 3 A.M., after the second Sunday in July, spent 24 hours in Eureka Springs, found Ellen better, left Wed. 6:30 P.M., arrived at home at Dermott, Thursday 3 P.M., left Friday 2 P.M. for Fountain Hill where I held a nine-day meeting, preaching day and night.

As a result of the meeting there, baptized three in July and in August and five in September. The day I was 78 years old, May 13, I went to Atlanta, Georgia, to the Southern Baptist Convention, the greatest convention. Arrived in Washington at 4 A.M. The 12th. Had a great convention, 8, 319 messengers enrolled. We were in session from the 12th to the 17th. I had a great time. Was shown many kindnesses by Congressmen Goodwin, Taylor Hudspeth of Texas, and Sen Joe T. Robinson of Arkansas, all of which was greatly appreciated by me.

Returned on the 20th just in time for the graduating exercises at Dermott, Arkansas, and heard the Valedictory by Vivian Skipper, which was good. My son's family at Warren were all sick from January to March with mumps and flu, but are all well now, having paid us a visit the first of May. I preached Sunday, the fourth Sunday at Blissville, morning and night. Have been preaching nearly every Sunday morning and night since October 22, baptized on the third Sunday in September two men, preached morning and evening at McArthur.

∞

Again the third Sunday in October, preached there and baptized one sister, the wife of one of the Brother Bonds I baptized September. Attended a reunion of Confederate soldiers at Camden, Arkansas, Bradley County, Arkansas. From Sept. 29th to October 1, I came home and left on the evening of the 2nd of October by way of Little Rock to Houston, Texas, for reunion of ex-confederate soldiers. Had a great time, but we are growing old and passing away day by day.

Appendices

Photographs

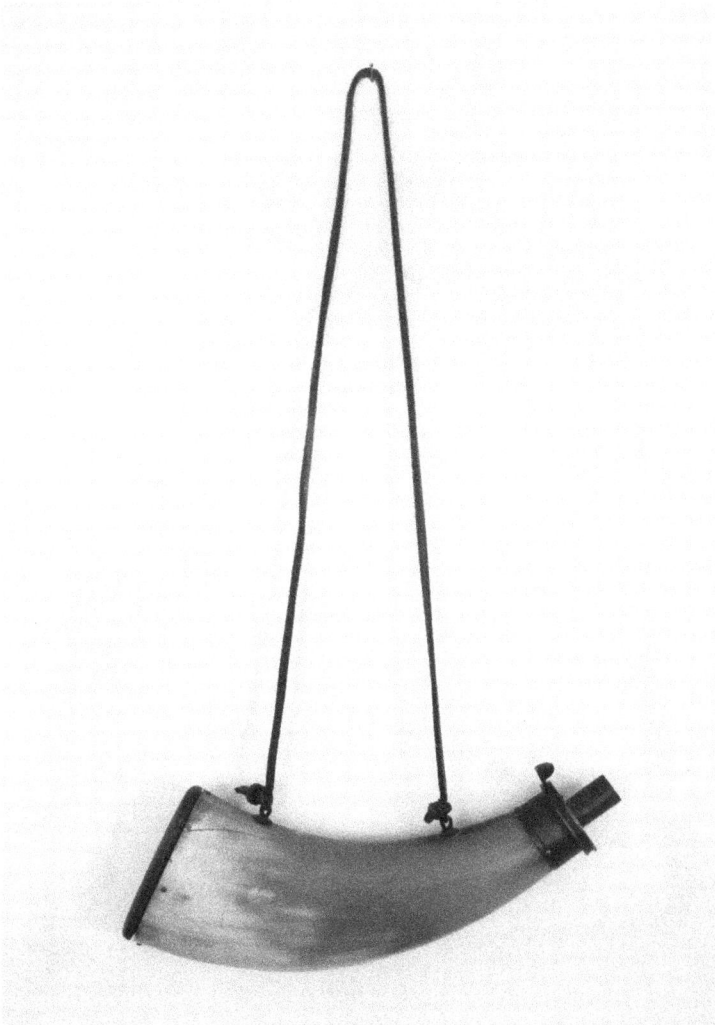

N. C. Denson's Civil War powder horn

Close-up view of the minie ball that struck N. C. Denson's belt buckle during the battle of Chattanooga

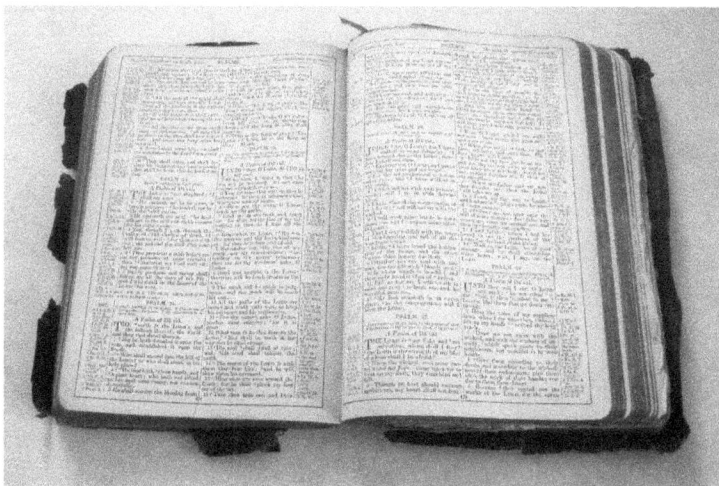

Reverend N. C. Denson's original Bible

New Mt. Pisgah Baptist Church, Sand Hill, Mississippi

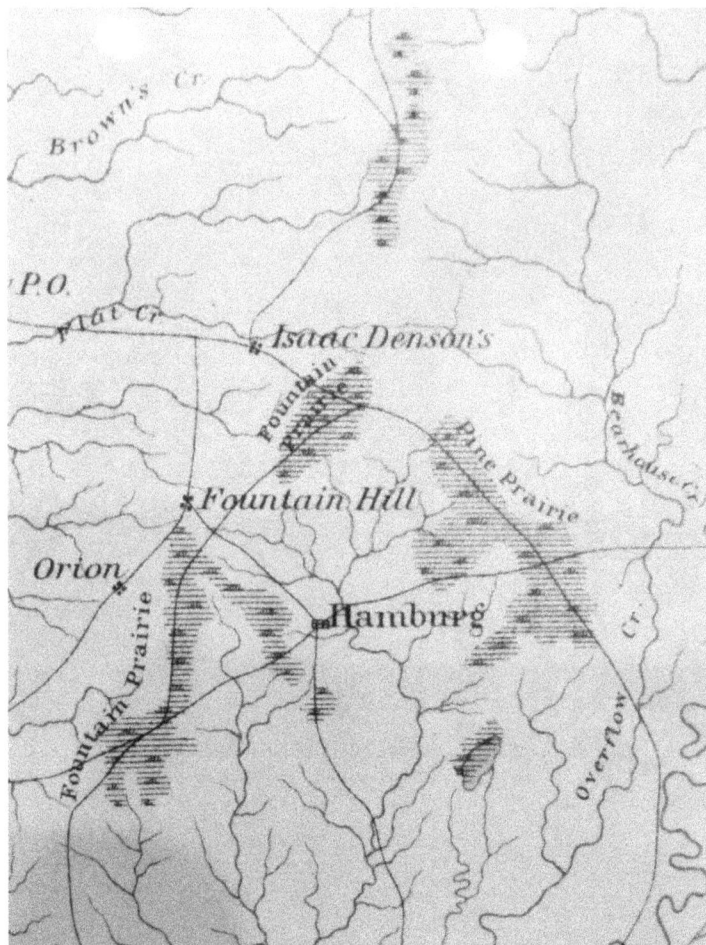

Isaac Denson's Arkansas homeplace about five miles from Fountain Hill. The house was also used as a court.

Isaac Denson, 1793-1875

Shadrick Denson, 1833-1892

Rufus King Denson, 1834-1887

William Albert Denson, 1871-1948

Wilson (Pete) Denson, 1915-1981

Gravesite, Mary Denson, 1805-1858, wife of Reverend William Denson, Sand Hill, Mississippi

Gravesite, Isaac Denson, 1793-1875, Sparks Cemetery, Lampasas, Texas

Gravesite, Shadrick T. Denson, 1833-1892, Sparks Cemetery, Lampasas, Texas

Gravesite, Reverend N. C. Denson, 1841-1929, Oakland Cemetery, Warren, Arkansas

Gravesite, Reverend N. C. Denson, 1841-1929, Oakland Cemetery, Warren, Arkansas

Gravesite, Reverend N. C. Denson, 1841-1929, Oakland Cemetery,
Warren, Arkansas

Gravesite, Rebecca Denson, 1845-1898, wife of Reverend N. C. Denson, Oakland Cemetery, Warren, Arkansas

Gravesite, William Denson, 1871-1948, and Fay Wilson Denson, 1886-1956, Oakland Cemetery, Warren, Arkansas

Gravesite, Scud Daniel, 1888-1948, and Lucy Denson Daniel, 1881-1949, Oakland Cemetery, Warren, Arkansas

Gravesite, Wilson "Pete" Denson, 1915-1951, and Sue Parrish Denson, 1924-1999, Oakland Cemetery, Warren, Arkansas

Gravesite, Jesse Denson, Sand Hill, Mississippi

Gravesite, Nathaniel Denson, Sand Hill, Mississippi

Gravesite, Charity Colson Denson, Sand Hill, Mississippi

Gravesite, Joseph "The Giant" Denson, Sand Hill, Mississippi

Gravesite, Araminta Smith Denson, Sand Hill, Mississippi

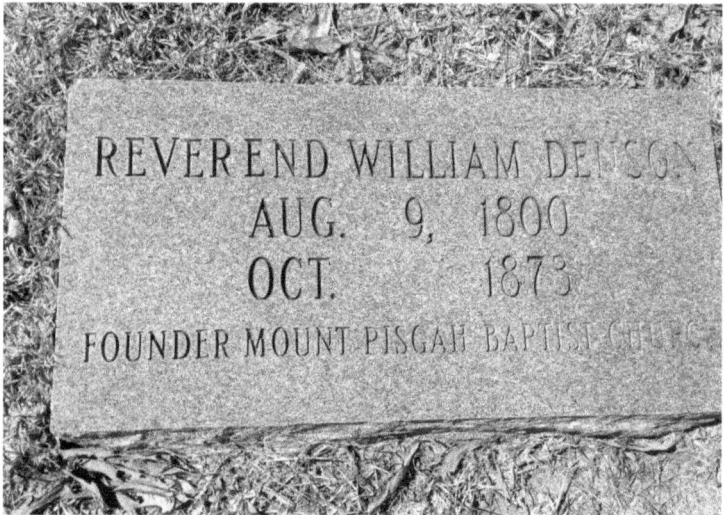

Gravesite, Reverend William Denson, Sand Hill, Mississippi

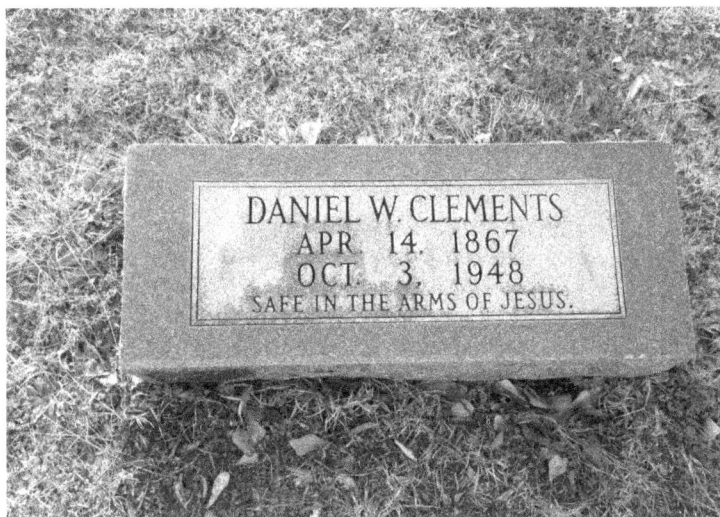

Gravesite, Daniel W. Clements, Oakland Cemetery, Warren, Arkansas

Gravesite, Emma Denson Clements, Oakland Cemetery, Warren, Arkansas

Gravesite, Nickolas Daniel Denson, Oakland Cemetery, Warren, Arkansas

JEROME
RELOCATION CENTER
1942 - 1944

ON FEBRUARY 19 1942 PRES. FRANKLIN
ROOSEVELT SIGNED INTO LAW EXECUTIVE
ORDER NO. 9066, INTERNING OVER 120,000
PERSONS OF JAPANESE ANCESTRY, AND
THIS ACT IRREVOCABLY CHANGED THEIR
LIVES. THE MAJORITY OF THESE PEOPLE
WERE AMERICAN CITIZENS. AS A RESULT
OF ALL THIS WARTIME HYSTERIA THESE
PEOPLE WERE FORCIBLY REMOVED FROM
THEIR HOMES ON THE WEST COAST OF THE
UNITED STATES AND ALSO IN HAWAII TO
BE INTERNED BY THE WAR DEPARTMENT
IN ONE OF THE TEN RELOCATION CENTERS
LOCATED IN THE INTERIOR OF THE U.S.A.
AT JEROME THERE WERE OVER 6,700
INTERNED FROM SEPTEMBER 1, 1942 AND
THROUGH JULY 1944, THESE TEMPORARY
SHELTERS WITH SHARED LIVING QUARTER
COMMUNITY DINING HALLS AND BATHING
FACILITIES WERE THE NORM. CONSTANT
ON-GOING SURVEILLANCE BY THE ARMY
SERVED AS A CONSTANT REMINDER OF
EACH RESIDENT'S CAPTIVITY AND LOSS OF
FREEDOM. THIS MEMORIAL IS DEDICATED
BY THE JEROME PRESERVATION COMMITTEE
AN ALSO THE JAPANESE AMERICAN CITIZEN
LEAGUE TO THOSE PERSONS OF JAPANESE
ANCESTRY WHO SUFFERED THE INDIGNITY
OF BEING INCARCERATED BECAUSE OF
THEIR ETHNIC BACKGROUND. MAY THIS
MONUMENT SERVE TO REMIND US OF ALL
THESE INCIDENTS AND INSPIRE US TO BE
MORE VIGILANT AND MORE ALERT IN THE
SAFE GUARDING OF THE RIGHTS OF ALL
AMERICANS, REGARDLESS OF THEIR RACE,
COLOR, OR CREED.

Jerome Relocation Camp marker

Obituaries

Minister 50 Years

𝒯he Rev. Denson was a Baptist minister for more than 50 years and was a leader in the work of organizing churches of his denomination in the state. He organized the Baptist churches at Dermott, Wilmot, Parkdale, Crossett, Arkansas City, Dumas, and McGhee [Wilmar, Blissville (later called Jerome), and McArthur]. For more than 20 years, he was a member of the Baptist State Mission Board.

He was born in Rankin County, Mississippi, May 13, 1841, but at the age of four moved with his parents to what is now Fountain Hill, Ashley County. He enlisted in Company K. Third Arkansas Regiment, Confederate Army, which was assigned to the Texas Brigade, Hood's Division and Longstreet's Army Corps, at Hamburg in March 1861. Twice cited for bravery in action, he served the entire war and was there when the Southern general surrendered to Gen. U. S. Grant.

Important Battles

𝒮ome of the important battles in which he fought were Sharpsburg, Greenbriar River, second battle of Manassas, Harper's Ferry, Chickamauga, Missionary Ridge, Lookout

Mountain, Spotsylvania courthouse, and Gettsburg. He was wounded in the battle of the Wilderness.

Following the Civil War, Mr. Denson settled in Warren, living there more than 30 years and serving as pastor of the Baptist church more than 12 years. He lived at Dermott 21 years and was pastor of the Dermott Baptist church 10 years.

Shortly before he died, he told his younger daughter much about what he thought were the meaningful moments of his life:

* First were the years following the early death of my father in 1848, leaving an eight year old. I was the oldest member of a young family. My grandfather, Isaac, and the remarriage of my mother to P. H. Baldy gave me the strength to keep his Denson family together.

* The second were the four years I spent in fighting for the Confederate States under General Robert E Lee.

* The third was Lee's surrender address to his men at Appomattox. I was close enough to hear Lee say his last comment to his men to return home and spread forgiveness and tolerance to all they could, to help bring as much reconstruction as possible to make one Great Nation. Those words could not be forgotten during almost every step I took from Appomattox to southeast Arkansas and as I visited with families of the brothers who would never come back home. General

Lee's words seemed to gain more strength and spiritual help than I thought I could provide. Somewhere between Appomattox and Fountain Hill, I had made my mind that the Lord had a path for me to follow for the rest of life: to dedicate the remainder of life to Jesus came as clear as a new morning.

Mr. Denson was one of the most beloved of Arkansas ministers, having thousands of friends in every walk of life throughout the state. His outstanding work in organizing churches and his membership on the Baptist Mission Board made him a leader of the denomination.

Pallbearers at his funeral were F. L. Johnson, Dermott; R. P. Stinson, Dermott; John Baxter, Dermott; John L. Carter, Little Rock; C. Hamilton Moses, Little Rock; and E. L. Compere, Hamburg. Honorary: Governor Parnell; Judge Carroll D. Wood, Little Rock; Dr. J. H. Estes, Little Rock; W. J. Raborn, Lake Village; W. H. Laphiew, Dermott; John Bain, Dermott; Dr. Isom, Dermott; T. L. Nichols, Parkdale; Dr. E. O. McDermott, Wilmott; R. H. Wolfe, Tiller; T. W. Gill, Gould; W.A. Stell, Portland; Carl Hollis, N.Y.; Dr. S. R. Herring, Henry Turner, F. M. Hickman, all of Warren.

Frank Denson

Reverend N. C. Denson

On last Sunday afternoon, Rev. N. C. Denson died at the Baptist State Hospital at the age of 88. We had already reported his serious illness. In fact, it was not so much illness as old age that caused his death. For several months, Brother Denson had been very feeble, and his vitality was gradually ebbing away. Therefore his death was not unexpected.

He is survived by two daughters, Mrs. W. S. Daniel of Little Rock, with whom he had for some time made his home, and Mrs. D. W. Clements of Gould; one son, W. A. Denson of Warren; two foster sons, Dixie Hannibal of Shreveport and Lee Hannibal of New Orleans; one stepson, Bruce Grubb of Dumas; and a stepdaughter, Mrs. C. F. Skipper of Dermott.

Brother Denson had a long and useful career, and it is doubtful that any other one man has ever been instrumental in the establishing of so many churches in the state. For many years, he specialized in the work of going to destitute places where there was no church, preaching, gathering converts, and organizing churches. He was a preacher for more than 50 years and organized the Baptist churches at Dermott, Wilmot, Parkdale, Crossett, Arkansas City, Dumas, McGehee, and other places.

He was born in Rankin County, Miss., May 13, 1841, but came with his parents to Ashley County, Ark., at the age of four. He was in many important battles in the Civil War, was wounded in the battle of the Wilderness, and was standing near General Robert E. Lee at Appomattox when he surrendered. He was for years a member of the State Mission Board of the Arkansas Baptist State Convention and was always a loyal and enthusiastic supporter of the convention's work.

He has finished his work and entered into rest, and we thank God for his ministry and for the blessed influence that has come from it and will continue through all time. What a meeting it must have been when he clasped hands with I. P. Eagle, J. B. Searcy, John Ayers, I. W. Conger, and many other fellow soldiers of Christ who had gone before to the glory land. May heaven's blessings abide on his loved ones.

The body was taken to Warren for burial, and the funeral was in charge of Pastor Otto Whitington, Immanuel Church, Little Rock, assisted by Pastor G. L. Boles of Warren, Carroll D. Wood, Jr., of Monticello, and I. F. Tull of Augusta.

Although it had been some years since Brother Denson moved away from Warren, he had lived there more than 30 years. An indication of the high esteem in which he was held by the people of Warren was the fact that flags at half mast were displayed in front of all business houses in Warren during the day and all such places were closed during the time of the funeral.

Baptist Advance
Little Rock, Arkansas
July 25, 1929

Nicholas Council Denson
May 13, 1841–July 21, 1929

The Rev. N. C. Denson, aged 88, has seen 50 years of service in the Baptist ministry in Arkansas. He retired from the pulpit three years ago, and for the past three years he has made his home with a daughter, Mrs. W. S. Daniel, 209 Vernon, Little Rock.

The Rev. Mr. Denson was born in Franklin [Rankin] County, Miss. At the age of eight, he came to Arkansas with his parents. When a boy of 17 years, he was baptized at Flat Creek Church in Ashley County, where his father, mother, and an uncle were charter members. After the close of the Civil War, he was ordained in the ministry at the same church.

As a member of the Third Arkansas Regiment of the Texas Brigade in Hood's Division, he was in every important battle of the War Between the States. He saw Stonewall Jackson killed and was present when Lee surrendered to Grant at Appomattox. He was in the thick of the fighting at Harper's Ferry, Gettysburg, Chickamauga, and Spottsylvania Courthouse, and was wounded in the battle of Wiedemer [Wilderness]. While on a scouting expedition on Lookout Mountain, he ran into a nest of Union soldiers on picket duty, and with the aid of his little party captured 13 of the enemy. In recognition of the deed, at Chicamauga, he was presented with the colors by Colonel Van H. Manning.

Following the close of the war, the young soldier returned on foot to his home in Ashley County. On the last day of his homeward journey he walked 50 miles.

He began his ministry in 1874 in southeastern Arkansas. Many of his charges were in out-of-the-way places, and to reach them, he traveled by horseback. Often, when the spring and fall rains had caused the creeks to overflow, he was forced to go by row boat.

For a number of years, he was a field missionary of the State Baptist Convention. He organized the Baptist churches at Dermott, Crossett, McGhee, Wilmot, Parkdale, Arkansas City, Wilmar, Blissville, and McArthur. He has been the pastor of churches at Warren, Hamburg, Dumas, Portland, Eudora, and Dermott. [According to the Fountain Hill Church records, he was also pastor there in 1912 and 1913.] He has been a member of the Baptist State Board for more than 34 years.

His parents were among the early settlers in southeastern Arkansas. In 1848 his father and an uncle surveyed the county of Ashley and located the county seat, which his father named Hamburg.

The Rev. Mr. Denson has not attended a church service in more than a year; however, he is in constant touch with the church through the radio. He always listens to the morning devotional service broadcast from the two local stations. The aged minister is partially deaf. He has second eyesight and often reads without the aid of glasses.

On May 13 he celebrated his eighty-eighth birthday. He was remembered by more than 100 of his former church members.

Arkansas Democrat

Nicholas Denson Grave Marker Text

*R*everend Nicholas Council Denson is buried with his first wife in the Oakland Cemetery at Warren, Arkansas. A tall obelisk spire type monument sits between the two graves with regular size markers on either side to mark the individual graves. The foot of the grave of Reverend Denson is marked by a metal cross.

East side of monument: *Denson*

West side of monument: *Denson*

South side of monument: *Asleep in Jesus*
   "Blessed are the dead who die in the Lord yea saith the spirit. That they rest fro their Labour and their works do follow them."
      Nicholas Council Denson
      Born May 13, 1841
      Died July 21, 1929
      Aged 88 yrs 2 mo 8 days
   He was a Baptist minister for more than fifty years. He organized more than fifteen churches.

North side of monument: *Safe in the arms of Jesus*
      Rebecca Wife of N. C. Denson
      Born Jan 9, 1845
      Died Aug 13, 1898

"Blessed are the dead, which die in the Lord: from hence forth, yea sayeth the spirit, that they may rest from their labours, and their works do follow them."

Smaller monument on south side of tall monument:
Father
He was a Confederate soldier for four years. He served under Gen. Robt. E. Lee. Surrendered with him at Appomattox.

Smaller monument on north side of tall monument:
Mother
She was a loyal daughter of the South.

Denson Genealogy

William Denson came to the Isle of Wight County, Virginia, in 1638, the first known Denson to arrive on these shores. He was brought here by the plantation owner Robert Pitt of Isle of Wight County, Virginia. It was here he worked seven years as an indentured servant. After this time, he married his wife, Frances. He bought 440 acres of land September 6, 1661, along the Nansemond River in Virginia. He came to this country because of religious persecution as an early Quaker following George Fox, the founder of The Circle of Friends Church. He continued as a Quaker and founded the Chuckatuck Meeting House, one of the oldest in the country. George Fox visited him several times, fostering the Quaker movement in the colonies. William was a well known Quaker who was the first to be elected to the Virginia House of Burgesses.

William Denson's son, James Denson, was born in Isle of Wight County and moved to North Carolina along the Pee Dee river and died in 1760. James's son, James II, also lived along the Pee Dee river. James II served under Colonel Abraham Sheppard as a private in the 10th regiment of the Colonial Army in the Revolutionary War. James II died in 1777. His son Nathaniel was born in Anson County, North Carolina.

Nathaniel (1770-1845) married Charity Colson (1772-1843) and began their family there. Their son Isaac was born there in 1793. Nathaniel and Casandra and Isaac and several of Isaac's brothers left North Carolina for Mississippi, but because of threatening Indians, the Densons first settled in Lawrence County, Alabama, in 1817. In 1827, they moved to Rankin County, Mississippi fighting Indians all the way and settled in the Pearl River swamp. One in the group, Capt. Bille J. Denson, was shot and killed by an Indian squaw with a poisoned arrow. After a period of living there, the family was successful in growing a large bounty of cotton and using the Pearl River to take it to market.

Isaac was already known for his success in fighting and defeating the British in the War of 1812. This victory in war had made the Pearl River usable for all Americans. Because of the Pearl river and the Denson success in growing cotton, this family became wealthy and influential, and this area in Rankin Co. became known as Densontown. The port was called Denson Landing, which is now on the bottom of the Ross Barnett Reservoir.

Isaac married Cassandra Grayson, and they had a son, Albert. Isaac moved his family out of Densontown, Mississippi, in the harsh winter of 1846-1847. Son Albert (then 30) and grandson Nicholas Council (then one year) accompanied them, along with several other Densons with their slaves and livestock. They settled down in an area just north of Fountain Hill, Arkansas, along Flat Creek.

Rev. N. C. and wife Rebecca had five children, five grandchildren, and five great-grand children.

1. Helen Hughes Denson
   b. 1867, Fountain Hill, Arkansas
   d. 1870, Fountain Hill, Arkansas

2. Carrie Bell Denson
   b. 1869, Fountain Hill, Arkansas
   d. 1870, Fountain Hill, Arkansas

3. William Albert Denson
   b. 1871, Fountain Hill, Arkansas
   d. 1948, Warren, Arkansas

   married Fay Wilson
   b. 1886, Monticello, Arkansas
   d. 1956, Warren, Arkansas

4. Emma Bradford Denson
   b. 1873, Warren, Arkansas
   d. 1951, Warren, Arkansas

5. Lucy Hughes Denson
   b. 1886, Warren, Arkansas
   d. 1949, Little Rock, Arkansas

Family of
Reverend Nicholas Council (N. C.) Denson

1. Nathaniel Denson
    b. 1770, Anson County, North Carolina
    d. 1845, Rankin County, Mississippi

2. Isaac Denson (son of Nathaniel Denson)
    b. 1793, Anson County, North Carolina
    d. 1860, Lampasas, Texas

3. Albert C. Denson (son of Isaac Denson)
    b. 1819, Alabama
    d. 1847, Fountain Hill, Arkansas

4. Nicholas Council (N. C.) Denson
    (son of Albert C. Denson)
    b. 1841, Gore Springs, Rankin County, Mississippi
    d. 1929, Warren, Arkansas

5. William Albert Denson
    (son of N. C. Denson)
    b. 1871, Fountain Hill, Arkansas
    d. 1948, Warren, Arkansas

    A. Albert C. Denson
        (son of William Albert Denson)
        b. 1913, Warren, Arkansas
        d. 1992, Odessa, Texas

    B. Wilson (Pete) Denson
        (son of William Albert Denson)
        b. 1915, Warren, Arkansas
        d. 1981, Warren, Arkansas

William Dillard Denson
(son of Wilson Denson)
b. 1949, Warren, Arkansas

Howell Rebecca Denson
(daughter of Wilson Denson)
b. 1956, Warren, Arkansas

C. Jane Rebecca Denson Tyler
(daughter of William Albert Denson)
b. 1917, Warren, Arkansas
d. 2010, Little Rock, Arkansas

William Daniel Tyler
(son of Jane Rebecca Denson Tyler)
b. 1946, Little Rock, Arkansas

D. Harry Yates Denson
(son of William Albert Denson)
b. 1927, Warren, Arkansas
d. 1993, Monticello, Arkansas

David Harry Denson
(son of Harry Yates Denson)
b. 1953, Crossett, Arkansas

Claudia Faye Denson
(daughter of Harry Yates Denson)
b. 1958, Crossett, Arkansas

E. Nicholas Daniel Denson
(son of William Albert Denson)
b. 1930, Warren, Arkansas
d. 1980, Warren, Arkansas

Denson Camp

At the Arkansas History Commission, I saw an exhibition on the Denson Camp. Included in this exhibit were original high school annuals of Denson High School and a letter cancellation postal stamp from Denson Camp, Arkansas. I did not know much about the Denson Camp but found the following articles referring to the Denson Camp. It should be noted that the number of Japanese in the camp (12,000) made it the sixth largest city in Arkansas at the time.

William D. Denson

Denson Relocation Center

In 1941 President Franklin Roosevelt recommended, at the request of the U.S. military, that relocation of Japanese Americans be made, especially from the west coast where they could represent a real danger to the war effort. For that reason, several areas were chosen in the interior of the United States. This included the Denson Camp at Jerome, Arkansas. This incarceration began on October 6, 1942, and closed on June 30, 1944. The Denson Camp held people from Los Angeles, Fresno, and Sacramento, California, and people from Honolulu, Hawaii. The camp included several thousand acres of wooded swamp land about 120 miles southeast of Little Rock.

A peak population of 8,497 was reached on November 2, 1943. This large Japanese community had a post office and newspaper. Denson High School was located in the internment camp. The camp residents had their own arts and crafts along with social gatherings. There were various Christian and Buddhist denomination services at Camp Denson during this period.

In 1944, the U.S. government closed the camp, and the evacuees were sent to the Rohwer Camp, where in 1945 a large number of Japanese Americans left for home in the West.

The Valedictorian speech of the Denson High school in 1944 summarizes the general feeling of those relocated to Camp Denson.

Valedictory
by Betty Kagawa

Editor's note: This speech shows that the lessons of forgiveness and tolerance Robert E. Lee hoped for his South were becoming a reality by men like Reverend N. C. Denson

This is truly an important occasion for the graduating class of 1944 of the Denson High School. In the years to come, each one of us will look back to this day with pride and pleasure as the first great goal of achievement attained.

At this moment, as we go through this ceremony, attired in our caps and gowns, we reminisce over the months of intimate association with our faithful teachers and classmates, and deep emotions stir within us.

We must realize the true significance of this occasion. It is, so to speak, a time to "take stock" of what we have gained and see where we stand. The days of childhood and early youth are over, and we approach the threshold of adulthood. Wherever we go from now, whatever we may do, we shall be judged not as children, but as citizens soon to assume a measure of responsibilities as such.

Some of us may be fortunate to enroll in a college presently and continue with higher education. Some may take up specialized vocational training, while others may seek gainful employment or assist their parents. Whatever we do, whether we pursue further studies or take up an occupation, we must show the results of what we have already gained, the lessons we have already learned, both in scholastic and in character development, during our high school years, now completed.

The world today is experiencing the agonies of a terrible conflict unprecedented in history. Although our own lives have been affected by the evacuation, and the restricted existence in this relocation center, we have not come in direct contact with the horrors of violence of war.

We are indeed proud to be citizens of this great country in which many opportunities are open to all. As citizens, we must recognize all our duties, obligations, and responsibilities. While we dearly love this country, nevertheless we realize that it does have many faults, that there are many existing conditions that must be improved—one of these deplorable conditions being racial prejudice. There are many worthy groups and organizations of fair-minded people that recognize the potential dangers of racial disunity within a country whose population is made up of peoples from all corners of the globe, and they have been working determinedly towards better understanding and harmony.

One of the chief advantages of a true democratic state is that each one of us as its citizens can play a part in bringing about changes for the better. It is up to us to win not merely a tolerant attitude but full acceptance and welcome in any community in the land. We must convince all with whom we come in personal contact that we are true Americans by our speech, thought, and actions; that we have the same high value and sense of loyalty burning within ourselves as any other American group.

The continuation of our education during the past year and a half has been of great value even though we were all transferred from the schools in which we originally enrolled and where we would have gone right through the prescribed number of years. Without a doubt, we all regretted the change, but it was a part of the circumstances of the war and had to be accepted. We are thankful for the services of our teachers, who have done their utmost in our interests to make up for the material shortcomings.

As the chosen valedictorian, speaking in behalf of my graduating classmates, I take this opportunity to express our deep-felt gratitude to each and all of our instructors, coaches, and supervisors for their untiring efforts. You have not only taught us ably and conscientiously, but have inspired us with your personal example, given us a thirst for true knowledge, guided us in learning to discriminate the worthwhile from the dross, in the appreciation of the good and the beautiful, taught us lessons in cooperation and fellowship, in patience and perseverance. We will never forget you nor what you have done for us, and will earnestly endeavor to show you the sincerity of our thanks by our actions in the years to come. For we realize that in your life careers as true teachers the greatest reward and source of satisfaction is to see outstanding success achieved by any of the students that you once taught. From among us may come some leaders of tomorrow, but in any event, we will try to be loyal, worthy, and useful citizens of the great country we all love—and a credit to you.

We bid you a warm and affectionate farewell.

Jerome (later Denson) Relocation Center
1942-1944
[Inscription on Dedication Marker]

On February 19, 1942, President Franklin Roosevelt signed into law executive order no. 9066, interning more than 120,000 persons of Japanese ancestry, and this act irrevocably changed their lives. The majority of these people were American citizens. As a result of this wartime hysteria, these people were forcibly removed from their homes on the west coast of the United States and also in Hawaii, to be interned by the War Department in one of the 10 relocation centers located in the interior of the U.S.A. At Jerome, there were more than 6,700 interned from September 1, 1942, through July 1944. These temporary shelters with shared living quarters, community dining halls, and bathing facilities were the norm. Constant on-going surveillance by the army served as a constant reminder of each resident's captivity and loss of freedom. This memorial is dedicated by the Jerome Preservation Committee and also the Japanese American Citizens League to those persons of Japanese ancestry who suffered the indignity of being incarcerated because of their ethnic background. May this monument serve to remind us of all these incidents and inspire us to be more vigilant and more alert in the safeguarding of the rights of all Americans, regardless of their race, color, or creed.

About the Author
William Dillard Denson, M.D.

illard Denson is a great-grandson of N. C. Denson. He was born December 17, 1949, in Warren, Arkansas, where he attended school and graduated Valedictorian in May of 1968. One month later, he began attending the Georgia Institute of Technology as a math major. Because of the field in which he was studying, he was offered a part in the work-study program at NASA. This allowed him to study his math at both Georgia Tech and the Manned Spacecraft Center in Houston, Texas. At Houston, he worked on the Apollo 8, 9, 11, and 13 programs. He applied to medical school at the end of his junior year in college and was accepted.

He began medical school in 1972 at the University of Arkansas for Medical Sciences College of Medicine, graduating in 1976. He completed a residency in adult neurology and psychiatry in 1980. He entered into private practice in adult neurology in 1980 in North Little Rock, Arkansas. He completed his written boards in neurology and psychiatry in 1981 and his oral boards in 1982. In March of 1989 he was elected as a Fellow with American Academy of Neurology.

In October of 1996, Dr. Denson retired after being diagnosed with multiple sclerosis. Since retiring, Dr. Denson has served on the Governor's board for People with Disabilities. He has also done research on his family genealogy. Dr. Denson has given much time working as a volunteer with the materials project for the Clinton Library, as well as in doing research for this book.

9780983899242